SEX

Get it. Want it. Have it.

For those that want it...
And those who *think* they don't.

MANDY MAGRO

First published 2017
EBook ISBN - 9780646969619
Print ISBN - 9780646969954

SEX, SEXTIONS and SEX-STEPS
Copyright by Mandy Magro

Except for use in any review, the reproduction or utilisation of this work in whole or in part in any form by any electronic, mechanical or other means, now known hereafter invented, including xerography, photocopying and recording, or in any information storage or retrieval system, is forbidden without the permission of the author.

This book is sold subject to the condition that it shall not, by way of trade or otherwise, be lent, resold, hired out or otherwise circulated without the prior consent of the author in any form of binding or cover other than which it is published and without a similar condition including this condition being imposed on the subsequent purchaser.

All rights reserved including the right of reproduction in whole or in any part in any form.

Published by
Mandy Magro
mandymagro75@hotmail.com
www.mandymagro.com

You've taken the first step to grabbing hold of the reins of your sex life – so good on you! Now it's time for the fun stuff…

LOVE, it's the universal language, but so is SEX.
And sex can be so much fun!

Throughout the ages, sexuality has been repressed and exploited. This book is about finding the happy medium, and getting your groove back in the bedroom, and on the couch, and on the kitchen bench…you get the picture. Everyone falls in love at some point in their lives. But, like it or not, love isn't enough to maintain a long-term relationship. Sorry! You have to have great sex too, and often! And no, ladies, once a month is not often. And men, women need more than the offer of a full body massage to be turned on - they know just what you're thinking. Sorry to burst your bubble.

Remember your first kiss where the world faded away and your entire body tingled? When you thought you could never feel so in love, so sexually attracted, so passionately head-over-heels ever again. If you could bottle that feeling and sell it, you'd be a squillionaire! Because sadly, in 99% of cases, once the "honeymoon" period is over and the reality of life kicks back in, that raging inferno of passion, the one where you wanted to tear each others clothes off with every opportunity you got, flickers out to more of a torch light when the batteries are going flat. Eventually, even that torchlight seems to go out, leaving the relationship in darkness. This leaves some partners frustrated and wondering why they're not "getting it" much anymore (other than their birthdays and at Christmas) and leaves others wondering if they're ever going to lust for sex again.

Don't lose faith. Not all is lost. You *can* have your cake (be in love) and eat it too (have mind-blowing, knock-your-socks-off sex). All it's going to take is for you, *and* your partner, to follow the Sex-Steps, Sextion by Sextion, and give every Sex-Step you choose to act out your full, whole-hearted effort. You ready for the ride of your life? Was that a yes? I thought so…great; it's the first step!

Guys, I'm sorry, but NO, you can't jump to the last few pages, skip all the intimacy stuff and try out the "hot sex" first - women just don't work like that. We're complex creatures (I can picture you nodding your head) and need a bit of effort to get our love juices flowing…there's nothing wrong with that. Ladies, our men need seducing too, so bear in mind each activity takes as much effort from you as it does from your man.

Think of each Sex-Step as foreplay, each activity building the sexual tension until the beautiful, mind-blowing finale. I promise, the end result will be well worth it! Because, let's face it, a union of two people in love without the addition of raunchy passionate intimacy is bound to fail, leaving both hearts broken and wondering where they went wrong. And before I continue…you're NEVER too old to rekindle the flames of passion.

Commitment, be it a whispered promise, or through marriage, doesn't have to spell the end of passion. Actually, the opposite is true. When you're fully immersed in the *feeling* of being in love, it's the most beautiful and indescribable experience. It's now you can totally trust your partner and do things you might not have done before. You can let your inhibitions go, knock down those protective walls, find intimacy in the newest of places, *and* have the kind of sex you've always dreamt of! By truly freeing yourself of your inhibitions you allow yourself, and your partner, to discover your true sexual nature - rekindling the flames of passion extinguished by taboos, daily routines and the pressures of modern day living. You'll both learn to treasure each sexual and sensual moment, naked *or* fully dressed. You'll become more sensitive, aware and loving towards your partner. And tahdah…they'll adore you for it. Then you'll "get it on" more often. See, not that hard huh? It's a win win situation for all when our mojos are alive and kicking. So, let's not beat around the bush (so to speak – ha-ha) and get cracking on the hot and steamy stuff…

SEX! What better way to express your feelings without saying a word? Or in some cases, screaming out in pure ecstasy while you orgasm hard, or talking dirty while you indulge each other? The human body has an enormous capacity for pleasure, so why not explore this?

We all want the best of both worlds, love *and* make-your-toes-curl sex. Why the hell not? We all deserve to be madly in love, *and* at the same time enjoying the pleasures of the flesh with the one we love. Take my word for it…you can have it all without having to change every aspect of your lives. Maintaining a healthy sexual relationship in this fast-paced world can be hard. Once there are little ankle biters thrown into the mix of our everyday responsibilities it can make having wild, passionate sex virtually impossible. When you do find time for sex? A quickie, snuck in late at night, when really, all you want to do is get a little more sleep, is not the most desirable scenario. Usually it's the man that benefits from these "quickies", leaving the woman unsatisfied and sexually frustrated.

There are many books and movies to guide you through what to do to save your sex life, but most of them are unrealistic and like a forest to manoeuvre through. How are you meant to banish the kids to their bedroom while you and your partner have a three-hour tantric sex session on the lounge room floor involving one hundred candles, a silk draped mattress, strawberries dipped in chocolate, and body-breaking sexual positions? Not going to happen! It may *sound* good but in reality you'd probably burn down the house, choke on a strawberry, or one of you would end up in hospital with a slipped disc. It never happens like it does in the movies.

With the help of this book you will discover many ways with my Sex-Steps, to re-ignite that raging inferno of passion once again. Because even though you may feel like your mojos have closed up shop and left for good, they're still there, lying dormant, dying to be awakened by your loving partner. And it's not that hard to do. There are just four simple rules you must follow to make the information you're about to read work to it's full sexual potential…

RULE 1

*You *must* choose to do at least 8 Sex-Steps from the 1st Sextion-Getting the Intimacy Back.

*You *must* choose to do at least 5 Sex-Steps from the 2nd Sextion - Exploring Bodies.

(Bear in mind the more Sex-Steps you can do the better!)

*With the 3rd Sextion - Ravishing Each Other - you can do as many as you like!

Each relationship is different to the next, and everyone is individual in their choices and life circumstances. Please choose Sex-Steps that feel right for you *and* your partner.

RULE 2

Don't force your partner to do anything they're uncomfortable with. Allow them to be themselves, but also try and push the boundaries together.

RULE 3

Do NOT skip Sextions. You must work your way through the different levels of intimacy to achieve sexual bliss.

RULE 4

Do NOT have sex until you've reached the third Sextion. This will teach you how to be intimate without the need for intercourse. It's a very *very* important factor.

With all the formalities done and dusted, let's get stuck into the nitty gritty of saving your sex life, and maybe even your relationship…

Getting the intimacy back without taking your clothes off. Yes, really!

Your Sexual Fantasy

To be able to complete this course you'll need to do this. Go on, you know you can! Just grab a piece of paper, and write down one of your sexual fantasies, or several, up to you. Make sure you get your partner to do the same. It can be as wild, or as tame, as you like. But, DO NOT, under any circumstances, look at what your partner has written. For now, it must remain a secret. Bear in mind that it should be something safe, and certainly not involving a third person. Then, together, place your folded up bits of paper in an envelope and seal it. Staple it down if need be so neither of you can sneak a peak at a later time, or if you like, place the bits of paper in a container and bury it in the backyard (as long as your four legged family member isn't going to dig it up)…just hide it wherever it tickles your fancy. You'll get to act out your fantasy later on, if you both choose to.

Cook Dinner Together

I know it might sound tedious, but it doesn't have to be. We all have to eat, so why not make it enjoyable? Choose a night that suits you both, preferably one where you don't have to get up for work the next day, and choose a meal that can be fun to cook. If you have children, try and call in a babysitter so you get some well-deserved alone time. Homemade pizzas or sushi are fun, or try and recreate that curry or stir-fry you both love so much. The choices are endless. Open a bottle of wine, crack open a few beers, or make a freshly squeezed juice…whichever you like. Now, put on some music and have some fun in the kitchen. Chat, flirt a little, and most importantly of all, relax in each other's company. Try and see each other for the person you fell in love with, away from all the stresses and responsibilities of life.

Turn off the Television

I don't care if the episode you've been waiting an entire season for is on, or the footy finale is playing, turn the box off, and turn each other on instead. Grab your swag, a blow up bed, an old mattress, or just a blanket, and go and lay out in the backyard underneath the stars. If you have young kids, wait until they've gone to bed, or if you have older ones, set them up with movies and junk food (yes, junk food is your saviour right now - so use it!). Grab some alone time for you and your partner. Take a bottle of wine, or a few beers, and just lay there, together. It may feel a little awkward at first, but eventually the conversation will kick in and so will the passion. Try not to talk about the kids, or work, just focus on each other. Maybe talk about what you used to do when you first met, where you used to go, what mates you hung out with, anything other than the usual. We have too many distractions in our lives, and this setting will take all those distractions away, allowing you both to connect on a deeper level than normal as you explore each other's minds. Which can be very sexy.

Love Notes

Do it the old fashioned way and grab a pen and paper, have fun and spell it out in magnetic letters on the fridge, or be inventive and write it on the mirror in the bathroom with lipstick. Whichever way, no matter how you choose to express it, use the written word to wow your partner and to remind them just how special they are to you. Nothing melts a heart more than reading how beautiful, sexy or amazing you are, and how much you're loved and cherished. We don't say this enough in our busy lives – and in turn can make us feel as though we're being taken for granted. Pop the note into their lunchbox, leave it on the bedside table, or slip it into their back pocket as you give them a kiss goodbye. It'll be a nice little surprise for later in the day. Or if you feel like being a bit naughty, tantalise your partner by leaving a little note somewhere private, telling them just what you'd like to do to them when you get your hands on them (at the end of this book of course – no jumping Sextions!). It may seem like a small thing to do, but it can mean the world. And your partner is the world, so why not let them know that?

Do it Together

No, not sex – well, not yet anyway. Whether it's yoga, salsa dancing, massage, cooking, cocktail making, pottery (the movie *Ghost* comes to mind) or a DIY class at Bunnings, go and do a class together. If you're feeling super naughty, maybe even a class in Kama Sutra or Tantric Sex – it will do wonders for your romps between the sheets. Whatever you choose to do, you'll be surprised how much more connected you both feel afterwards. To show interest in your partner's hobbies/passions is another way to show them how much you love them. This will make them want to drag you off to the bedroom so they can have their wicked way with you – oh yeah baby! (But hold your horses until the end of the book, okay?) Don't wait a minute longer, get on the phone, or online, and book that class now. What have you got to lose?

Movie Date

What better place to go with your partner then the cinema. You get to sit in a dark room, snuggled up to one another (yes you must do this), with plenty of opportunity for sneaky touches and kisses. Oh yes please! Try and treat it like a first date, and let the outside world and your endless responsibilities fade away for the next coupe of hours. Both of you deserve time-out, together. Afterwards, if you can, take the opportunity to go for a coffee, a drink at the local bar, or a cheeky dessert at one of your favourite restaurants. As long as it's somewhere cosy and clam so you can talk – but not about the kids, or the bills, or even work, make sure you talk about things like the movie you just watched or dream destinations for a future holiday together. Keep it light, fun and interesting.

Men, Strap on those Aprons!

Speak to almost any woman and she'll agree that it's damn sexy seeing their man whipping up a storm at the stove or hanging off the end of the vacuum cleaner. It's the perfect example of actions speak louder than words, especially if the man tells his beautiful queen to go and put her feet up while he does it. Ladies, your heart is gushing just thinking about it, right? And why wouldn't it? To see a man taking charge in what predominantly is a woman's domain is irrefutably hot.

Guys, it will make your lady purr with hungry desire to get you naked – winning! (But once again, not until the end of this book – put that thing down!) If you want to be a little naughty, just wear an apron and nothing else, so your lady can have a good perv at your butt – food for thought. There's the potential to have so much fun with this. So come on you sexy beast of a man, take over the housework for a little while – you've got this!

Ladies, put on that Lingerie!

If you've got it stashed away in your cupboard, beneath everything else that's accumulated over the years, get it out and dust it off. If you don't own any, or the pieces you have are falling to bits or out-dated, go out and buy yourself some. You deserve to feel sensuous. You're a sexy carnal woman so it's justifiable to embellish that gorgeous body of yours! And your man will love you for it. Lingerie is like a secret weapon, and not only for the lucky person admiring you in it. It will make you feel super sexy, and powerful. Whether your style is burlesque, simplistic, girl-next-door, virgin-white, or dominatrix, (suspenders, garters and stockings OH MY!) own it and turn that man of yours on like a house on fire. It doesn't have to be blatant either. You can slip it on beneath your uniform - making sure your man sees you getting dressed for your day at work, or you can go all out and wear it around the house or to bed (dependent on whether you have kids in the house, of course). Either way, remember it's not to be ripped off in hungry ravenous sex just yet – that fun is still to come. Excuse the pun!

Spirited Fun

Put that laptop down, turn off the television and your mobile phone, and snap that inner child of yours back into action! Play a board game, go to a theme park, go for an ice-cream, run around the backyard in the sprinkler, play hide and seek, chase each other along the beach as you try and avoid being dunked under a wave, go to your local Jump Mania and bounce them trampolines like you damn well mean it (just be careful you don't break a limb in the process). Carefree play relieves stress, brings excitement to the relationship and builds intimacy – a win win situation overall. It may feel a little foreign at first, but do your best to let go, be silly, be vulnerable, and escape from the confinements we place on ourselves with being responsible adults. Rough and tumble play is a great way to touch your partner without it having to be sexual, and this strengthens your bond in an extremely fun way. Pillow fights are awesome fun, just for an example. It may feel a little forced at first, but persist, and before long you will be racing around like a pair of kids laughing like you haven't laughed in ages. Go on, I dare you to try this!

10

Gifts

It doesn't have to be a Porsche, or expensive jewellery. It's the thought that counts. Coming home with a bunch of flowers or a box of chocolates for your partner speaks volumes. If they're not into either of these things, make it up as you go – wine, candles, a nice bottle of scotch, perfume, aftershave, a couple's massage voucher, their favourite cake from the bakery, takeaway to save them having to cook – the choices are endless. The fact you went out of your way to get your partner something they love will melt their heart every time. Promise! If you're on a really tight budget, it doesn't have to be a gift that costs anything – picking a few flowers from your garden (or the neighbours if you don't have any flowers in yours), or writing out a voucher to give them a massage or a foot rub, is just as sweet and evocative as buying them something. Little things can mean so much.

Arousing Aromas

Essential oils can boost your low libido. Yes, really. So get that oil burner cranked up and make your house smell of everything that awakens you both to feeling sensual. Beautiful scents stimulate sexual arousal and put you in the mood to be affectionate towards your partner – it's a proven scientific fact. Frankincense, ylang ylang, musk, rose, and sandalwood are among the best, but it's personal choice and if you find an essential oil you like better, use it. Scented candles also work, but make sure they're quality ones made with essential oils. Nag Champa incense is equally alluring, and you can grab a packet for a couple of dollars from your local health food shop. There are no hard and fast rules with scents. This is all about doing what appeals to both of you. Make a trip to the shops and spend a bit of time picking out a few oils or candles you'd like to try out. It will be time well-worth spent together.

Breakfast in Bed

A lazy Sunday spent in bed with your partner, eating breakfast and taking your time to begin the day, is always a winner. If you have children, there's nothing wrong with giving them a bowl of cereal or some toast, and popping them in front of the television for a little while. They'll actually have fun doing this, while you and your partner spend some stolen time together. To make your occasion as hot and special as ever, there are a few things to keep in mind. Foods that are sticky or drippy are out, unless you want the arduous task of having to change the sheets. Stick to what you know, and what you like to cook – now's not the time to try and become the next Michelin star chef. Don those pyjamas, fluffy robes, or silky negligee and boxers, and enjoy each others company as you start your day off slowly rather than diving from the bed with a millions things to do.

Dance

Whether it's getting dressed up and going out, in your pyjamas in the lounge room with the lights down low, or out on the back lawn beneath a blanket of stars (while the kids are running amok in the house), just grab your partner and hold them close. It can be slow dancing to your favourite love song, jiving and swinging to a blast from the past, or head banging to your favourite heavy metal band – the choice is yours. Bearing in mind, that the closer you are, the more intimate it is, and the more intimate it is, the more fuel there will be to ignite the building fire between you. Dancing hip to hip can be so very sexy, so make the most of it. Scientific fact - dancing naturally increases your endorphins, making you happier and more relaxed, and in turn makes you more open to closeness from your partner. So go on, lose your inhibitions and dance like nobody is watching!

Sexting

Talking dirty can be extremely hard, awkward, and potentially embarrassing when said face-to-face, but texting, well, that opens the playing field and your scope to say exactly what you like. It also gives you time to not have to come up with something hot and erotic in the heat of the moment. It may feel weird at first, but remember, it doesn't matter what you say, just as long as it's something that will turn your partner on. Put ideas in their head of what you'd like to do to them when you're at the third Sextion of this book. Tell them how sexy they are. Remind them of the things you used to do that you want to rekindle. Tell them what you're wearing, or not wearing for that matter…you can have loads fun with this one. Opening the door for this kind of talk in a relationship will repay you both tenfold once you get each other naked. Trust me! So go on, take the plunge and do it.

15

Flirt with Each Other

If you think flirting is for when you first meet someone…wrong! It's an essential part of foreplay in a long-term relationship. Without it, your sex life will be very dull indeed. It reminds your partner what you love about them, and keeps the romantic spark alive outside of the bedroom. Best of all it gets your subconscious mind thinking about ripping each other's clothes off and that's what we're aiming for…right? A cheeky glance, unashamedly perving on each other, a compliment alone or with other people, a stolen bum squeeze, a hug, a kiss, holding hands when your out and about or on the couch, or just saying something sexy that makes them wish they could get you alone right then and there – the options are endless and up to your imagination. Whichever way you choose to do it, flirting is like kindle to a fire – you need it to keep the flames alive between you.

Snuggle

An easy one…but very important to keep a loving relationship alive. Be honest. How long has it been since you've really snuggled up to each other? If it's recently, good on you, and keep it going. But if you can't remember, this one's unquestionably for you both to conquer. Instead of sitting at opposite ends of the couch to watch television at the end of a busy day, or having an imaginary line down the middle of the bed with each of you confined to a particular side, scoot over to one another and snuggle like you mean it. There is so much to be said for being in each other's arms – a very simple yet powerful tool to intimacy. To rest your head on your partner's chest, and feel their heartbeat against your cheek, or to just feel like you're home within their arms, is beautiful. It will teach you to touch without it needing to lead to sex – that bit will come soon enough. For now, just enjoy the feeling of being close to one another.

Date Night

Date night is a ritual you should regularly indulge in – be it weekly, fortnightly or monthly. It should be a flagged time on your calendar, without question or excuse. Quality one-on-one time is essential to keep the spark alive and it can do wonders in taking you back to your days of courtship. If you have children, call in the babysitters, and take time out for you both. You deserve to! Life is for living, no just existing. Go out to dinner, grab some takeaway and go and sit on the beach or at a park, go and see a live band, or just go to your favourite coffee hang out - do whatever it is you both enjoy doing, together. Reminisce about old time, happy times, times that remind each other of the person they fell in love with, and try and avoid the daily chit-chat about work, kids and the mortgage. As you begin doing this, you will look forward to the next time, and the next. It will become a part of your relationship that you are unwilling to miss. And rightly so.

Sensual Kiss

Soft and tender, or full and passionate, the kiss is profoundly the most intimate sexual exchange between lovers without needing to take your clothes off. It awakens the erotic responses of the body and rekindles the flames of passion. For now, don't use it as a prelude to a bigger event (hungry tear-your-clothes-off-sex), and have no specific goal other than being intimate with one another. Allow your tongues to play with one another's. Swirl, nibble, lick and suck. Build the crescendo by running the tip of your tongue over your lover's lips, stopping to gently tease your lover into wanting more of where that came from. Lose yourselves into one another, allowing everything else in the world to disappear, if only for these few brief toe-curling moments. Kissing is beautiful, and should be done often.

Exploring one another's bodies, without the expectation of sex Yes, it's possible, and very seductive!

The Sensual Massage

This is going to take a dedicated commitment to not manipulate the situation – don't break the rule of no sex before you reach the finale. I'd recommend wearing underpants; otherwise the temptation might be too much. Stay resilient - we're almost there… Touch is the language of love, and a massage is the best way to relax your lover and reconnect on a physical and emotional level. With sensual massage, giving is receiving. It's the perfect way to stoke the inner fires of passion and desire, without expecting an end result (sex). Create your space. Use low soft lighting, or candlelight, and play some nice background music. Have a nicely scented massage oil and warm it up in your hands before applying it to your partner's skin in smooth, flowing strokes. Alternate between softer and deeper pressures while you explore your lover's body as if it were the very first time. This can be extremely arousing, for both of you. Become totally absorbed in them, re-learning where they liked to be touched and which parts of them evoke moans and sighs. This is very important information for later, in Sextion 3.

Get Steamy

Showering is usually a time where you can escape from the world and the noisiness of the house for a few bliss-filled moments, so why not do it together? It's just as sexy as skinny-dipping, only far more intimate. Light a candle and turn off the blinding overhead light, play some music if you can, and strip down until you're gloriously naked. Run the bath or turn on the shower, and get ready to turn each other on at the same time. Sink into the bath and snuggle into one another. Or stand in the shower and allow the warm water to cascade over you while you share a kiss. Try to remain gloriously uninhibited as you fall into the moment together.

Lather your hands up and wash your partner's body, from head to toe, avoiding the places in-between that might tip you over the erotic edge – you can always divulge in this once you've reached Sextion 3. Use this time to get to know each other on an intimate level without the need for an end goal – it will strengthen your bond tenfold. These few moments together will make the world of difference on your path to a better sex life.

The Spontaneous Kiss

When they least expect it, grab your partner and kiss them like it's the first time your lips have ever met. Catching them off guard makes it all the more exciting, for both of you. Imagine your lips might never meet again to build the hunger. Do it like you mean it. Kiss them like they loved to be kissed. Entice them into a swirling of tongues while you pull them nearer, closing any distance between yourselves. Own the kiss. Take their breath away. Make their knees buckle. Make them want you like they've never wanted you before. Do this at home, walking along the street, or in the middle of a busy shopping centre – the possibilities are endless. It all depends on your level of adventurous spirit. Go on, you know you want to. Live in the moment, together.

Feather Tickler

For this Sex-Step you both need to be naked, and fully committed to not going the entire distance. This is all about exploring one another, and divulging one another, without doing the deed. You need to learn how to *want* each other again, without expecting anything in return. Choose who's going to be the giver first, and then you can swap roles later on. Once you're stripped down, the receiver needs to lay down somewhere comfortable, and private. This is brilliant when your partner is blindfolded, as it makes for a more tantalising time – but of course this choice is yours. Feather ticklers are sensuous luxurious tools to awaken your lovers touch receptors, and can easily be ordered off the internet to save you going to a sex shop. Straddling your partner, or sitting beside them, brush the feather all over their skin, following through with a few kisses along the way. Linger on the breasts, nipples, and nether regions for as long as they can take it. Heighten your lover's experience by caressing, kissing and blowing cool air over them as you do. Be inventive, be fun, be uninhibited, and you'll enjoy this more than you imagined.

Eye Contact and Heartbeats

This is quite an intense Sex-Step. It can be extremely revealing, and allow walls that have been built to crumble. If done openly, it can connect you on a very intense level, and sometimes even bring up hurts that needed to rise to the surface so you can both love each other more openly. Choose a time that you will not be disturbed – aid this by turning off the phones and locking the front door. Sitting opposite each other, so your knees are just touching, take each other's hands and rest your arms down. Meet each other's eyes, and maintain long-lasting contact for 4-5 minutes, or just as long as you can handle. Use a timer if that helps, so you're not looking away to check your watch. Your eyes are the windows to your soul, and by doing this exercise you're connecting with your lover on a very powerful level. Don't speak, and just let your eyes do the talking. Try and stay relaxed, and blink as many times as you need, but just don't break the eye contact. Once this is completed, while still remaining silent, each of you raise a hand to your lover's chest, close your eyes, and really try and feel their heartbeat against your palm.

Sexy Photos

This can be so much fun, so allow your inhibitions to melt away as you indulge each other in flirty, naughty photos. It doesn't have to be the perfect shot of you strutting your stuff like some nude model. In fact, you can be fully clothed if you choose to be. Be cheeky, be inventive, and let your imagination run wild. Ladies - take a pic of your butt in those cute little denim shorts, in your favourite bra and panties, your cleavage, your nipple, or just throw caution to the wind and do whatever takes your fancy at the time. Embrace being a woman in all its glory! Men - show your sexy minx your chest, or the bit just above your jocks that tapers down to what will be their favourite place in the whole wide world at the end of this book, or your butt, or go the whole hog and show it all in hard tremendous glory. As with everything in this book, it's personal choice. Just please be respectful and keep the pictures to yourself. This is about the two of you, not others.

Sleeping Naked

What better way to end your day than being skin-on-skin with your partner? It's freeing, both physically and psychologically, and helps to build trust between you. So, get those daggy polka-dot pyjamas off, or the boxers that say how damn hot you are, and do it in the nude. Enough already with the clothes we have to wear day in day out! Embrace the privacy of your bedroom (or house if you have no children wandering about) and strip on down. Snuggling into one another, skin on skin, is erotically beautiful. It releases the hormone oxytocin, lowers your heart rate, and reduces blood pressure. All of this increases the feeling of comfort, and relaxation. It's been scientifically proven that sleeping naked and cuddling with your loved one improves your health…so get onto it. Self-control in this situation is imperative, though. You don't want to spoil the ending, do you? Why race to the finishing line when you can enjoy the journey along the way? Simply revel in having nothing dividing you both, and enjoy the sensation of being so close. Just make sure you lock the bedroom door if you have kids!

Pleasuring Yourself

If you've never done this before, then what are you waiting for? Free yourself from the taboos of masturbation, and unbolt the narrow-minded shackles of society. It's natural, our given right, and something we should all master the act of. By learning to pleasure your own body, you will discover how and where you like to be touched. Then, you can pass this knowledge onto your partner. Yay! While exploring, don't hurry to climax. It's not a race to the finishing line, but a journey of euphoric discoveries. Take all the time you need to appreciate the sensations that come with masturbation. Once you reach the summit, move, sigh and moan as you surrender your body to waves of pleasure. You're allowed to enjoy it! And once you've mastered this yourself, it can be extremely hot to do this in front of your lover. If you're game – which I know you are.

Spend a Day Naked

(But cook bacon at your own risk)

It's time to break free, take off the camouflage, and be the real true authentic you! You don't have to be a part of some nudist camp to spend the day in the buff. As much as it's fun for you, it can be scintillatingly teasing for your partner too. Not an easy feat if you have children about, but not impossible. Call the babysitters in and take a day, or even better a weekend, out for yourselves. As I keep saying, you deserve to. Teaching yourself to be at ease in your birthday suit can feel a little strange, but it's well worth it. It will make you comfier around one another, and more confident within yourself. Grab the chance to take naked photos of each other, or just curl up on the couch and watch a movie. The scope of possibilities is endless. Whatever you do, you're going to have less laundry, and that's a big plus! And on the serious side, it will bring you even closer together.

Ladies, (and men) Go Commando

Ditch your panties, or jocks. It's comfy, liberating, great for sneaky hands-on moments and super dooper sexy. Feeling the air swirl around up there is pleasuring within itself, let alone letting your partner know you're partially naked, especially if you're out and about. Live a little, leave your inhibitions in your draw and be a little risqué. It will give you a rush, being bare. And then flaunt it, work it, own it - you got this! Whisper you're panty-less in your partner's ear, and let the fireworks start. A sneaky fondle at the kitchen sink, an oops-I-dropped-something-and-need-to-pick-it-up-moment, or deciding to announce it (quietly) while out having a coffee or a romantic dinner, makes for some very provocative moments. Feeling your partner's hand slide up your thigh beneath a table is exhilarating, especially when they reach the pleasure zone. So go on, throw caution to the wind and try this one out. You'll both love it!

Ravishing one another with your clothes off.
Yes, Yes, Yes... finally!!!

Sex Toys

In a long-term relationship foreplay can easily become choreplay, and lovemaking can become tedious and predictable. We don't want that! Sex toys spice it up, to a scorching level, adding enjoyment to your bedroom sessions. And ladies, by incorporating a vibrator into the mix, your chance of reaching an orgasm increases considerably and puts less pressure on your partner to make it happen. Now that's got to be a massive draw card! From lubricants that tingle and warm, handcuffs, leg clamps, edible massage oils, to vibrators with a multitude of functions, there's an endless array of toys to choose from. It's all up to your personal choice. Vibrating love rings (especially ones that have testicle stimulation) are brilliant, giving you both equal pleasure. Ladies, glide it down his shaft with plenty of lube, climb on top of your man, and be blown away by the clitoral stimulation as you slide up and down. Guys, it will prolong your erection and give you an extremely powerful orgasm. So what are you waiting for? If you haven't already got a stash in the bedside draw, race into an adult store and get shopping with your partner.

2

Porn

Going solo with porn is fine, if that's what you like to do, but why not share the experience together? It's not as bad as society makes us think. It doesn't have to be hard-core (unless this tickles your fancy of course), soft porn is just as effective.

It can be a useful way to increase arousal, and to introduce new ideas into your boudoir. You don't have to go to a shop to get yourselves some either, porn now readily available with the click of a button. It's a great way to introduce the fantasies you're maybe too shy to share with your lover, and in turn get the engines revving. Erotic images can create closer intimacy, and pave the way to a deeply trusting, open relationship with one another. No longer do you have to worry if your other half is watching it when you're not around – you can do this together. Fantasy is all part of a healthy sex life, and porn just brings it to the forefront so you can share it with one another. For those of you that haven't experienced doing this together, it can be quite daunting, but trust me, once you ease yourselves into it you will love it.

Breathing In

Inhale. Exhale. You both do this all day long without giving it a second thought. But by becoming more aware of your breath, you can become more tuned into one another, and more turned on by one another too. Inhaling and exhaling in synch with your lover is a very simple yet extremely powerful way to strengthen your emotional connection. So when you can steal a few quiet moments lie on your side, facing each other. Wrap your arms and legs around one another so you're snuggled in tight. Press your lips into one another's as if you're about to have a hungry tongue pashing session. Now, breathing in and out, try to synchronise your breathing so that when you lover breathes out, you breath him/her in, and then in return they do the same for you, so both of you are essentially breathing each other in, deeply. Once you've got the rhythm down pat, imagine melting into each other. It's beautiful. This will increase arousal, and create a deeper connection.

Heightening the Senses

Sight, smell, taste, touch and hearing – every one of these senses can be used to build arousal, and a deeper connection between you. By heightening your senses, you open the door to greater sensory perception and potentially more intense orgasms. Oh yeah baby! So, pop on some nice background music. Grab some food easy to feed each other – fruit, chocolates, or even nuts. Pick some scents to let your lover breathe in – essential oils, perfume, aftershave, soaps. Round up some ice to use on them or to cool your tongue down for intense licking. Some of your sex toys – vibrators, feathers, silk, body oils to rub all over them, and finally something to use as a blindfold. Everything I've mentioned here are only examples – you can choose what you wish and even come up with ideas of your own. Let your imagination run wild and grab whatever appeals to you both. Choose who's going to be the active, and the passive, and you can swap half way through. Pop the blindfold on, and let the fun begin.

Dew Drop Kiss

Time to lay down ladies and let your partner pleasure you. Pop a pillow beneath your hips, if you like, as this makes you more comfortable and gives your partner great leverage. With over 6000 nerve endings, there are endless indulgences to be bestowed when done properly. Guys, imagine your tongue is like a feather at first. You must start off in a teasing manner and build the anticipation of your lips meeting her most sensitive part – because it makes it *more* sensitive when you do this. Get her gripping the sheets and begging you for mercy before you succumb to her desires. You're in control, so make the most of it. Start with her inner thighs, licking and kissing, and work your way upward and inward. Once you've reached her sweet centre, there's no better way to explain it but to mimic licking and sucking an ice cream. Promise, you'll get her writhing in erotic pleasure in no time. Slow licks firstly, upwards, and downwards. Bring your mouth down, covering it all. Slowly slide your tongue inside her, and then savour the upward stroke before you pull out and circle the clitoris. Build the crescendo by picking up the pace, flicking, and licking and sucking – being mindful of what she likes the most. Vibrators can also be loads of fun combined with the pleasures of your tongue, so if you're up for it, use one. Bring her to the edge and enjoy the sound of her breathless all because of you, before she tumbles into the abyss of a mind-blowing orgasm.

Penis Pleasuring

Turn the lights down low and get that hunky man of yours on his back. It's time to take charge and pleasure him. If done with desire it will amp up your own arousal. First things first - we're not jackhammers ladies, so take it slow - your man will love it and so will you. Kneeling before him, caress his testicles lightly and provocatively. Run your fingertips over the tip – there are a bundle of fabulous nerve ends there. Take his erection in your hand. Start at that yummy glorious head and run your tongue ever so slowly around the top. Breathe over it, lick it, run your mouth over it, but only let your lips touch lightly. Tease it out. Make his knuckles white from gripping the sheets. Make sure there's heaps of lubrication before you slide your mouth down, taking him in inch by glorious inch as you tighten your grip around the base of his shaft (only go down as far as comfortable – gagging not a turn-on for either of you). Then, as you come up for air, rub up and down his shaft, at the same time sucking the head in a rhythmic motion. Give him devilish looks or talk dirty if you're up for it. Men love it. If your mouth or jaw gets achy or tires, rest for a few moments by kissing his inner thighs, as he will love that too. When you bring him to that blissful edge, swallowing can be such an intense experience for you both, so if you can, do it.

Male G-spot

Crank the aircon, because things are about to get mighty hot. This is the ultimate pleasure house of the body, and when tantalized and teased, you'll take his pleasure to amazing heights. Quite possibly ones he's never been to before. The male g-spot builds tension throughout his entire body and stimulates blood flow to his genitals, intensifying his orgasm tenfold. The magic button is a walnut-size gland under his bladder. Rest two fingers against the soft skin between his genitals and anus, and you've found it. By applying pressure here, you're incidentally rubbing his G-spot. This is a perfect thing to do when pleasuring him orally. When he's close to an orgasm apply pressure rhythmically (one press every second) until he reaches the ultimate summit. There's a deeper way to do this and that's going backstage, but only if your man approves. If he does, apply some lube and insert your finger 2 inches in. Curl it forwards until you feel a round bulb of soft tissue – that's his prostrate. *Very* lightly swirl your finger over it and watch him gasp in pleasure.

Female G-spot

A sacred spot that once discovered will never be ignored again. EVER. You can find the promised land just inside the front wall of the vagina. It will feel like a small patch of knobbly tissue about 2 inches in – found easier when aroused. Like the clitoris, when stimulated, it can bring you to mind-blowing orgasms faster than penetrative sex. When climaxing from G-spot stimulation, it's deep, and oh so good! You can't just hit the g-spot and climax, though, it takes a bit of work – but the effort is well worth it. Curved vibrators are perfect but just make sure you're using plenty of lube. Combine this with some oral stimulation, and guys, your woman will writhe in ecstasy. Another way to rouse this mind-blowing spot is to climb on top ladies and ride him like you mean it. While in control you can angle his penis to rub at the prefect spot. And when you've found it, let your man know so he stays there as you climb to euphoria. Popping a pillow beneath his hips can help, as the position makes it easier. An alternative is with your man behind you, his legs positioned *outside* of yours, and for him to lean forward as he thrusts while tilting your bum upwards.

Do it in the Open

It might not be for everyone, but it's such wickedly naughty fun. Brook Shields did it in Blue Lagoon, and boy oh boy did that rev people's engines in all the right ways. And there's a good reason for it. Having sex in nature is as primal as you can get, and a wonderful aphrodisiac. Look at it like eating out at a restaurant over eating at home. Not so bad, right? It shouldn't be blatantly obvious, like in the middle of a shopping centre at peak hour. There are plenty of spots you can indulge in freeing yourselves of inhibitions without being charged for indecent exposure. Find a love-nest that's off the beaten path, as far away from other people as possible. Your backyard is perfect, or out in the middle of the bush, by a river, in the ocean, or on a deserted beach – wherever tickles your fancy and you're not going to get busted. It's the thrill of getting caught that spices things up, but actually achieving that is not a desirable way to cease a raunchy lovemaking session. If you're going to do this, be committed. Throw yourselves into it, and throw those inhibitions we all have far off into the horizon.

Penis Pulsing

Very satisfying, and oh so addictive…enjoy some hot foreplay to get you both into the mood. Once you're ravenous, ladies, climb on top of your man. Make sure you're nice and wet, or use plenty of lube. Slowly, slowly, side him inside of you. Then stop. Lean over and kiss him. Make him wait. Make yourself wait. Prolong. Build the sexual tension. Sitting back up, use your pelvic floor muscles - relax and contract them. This will get your vaginal walls to embrace his erection. Do this for a few minutes, either sitting up and teasing him, or leaning forward and kissing him. Whatever feels right for you. Then, raise your butt upwards, teasingly slowly, stopping right at the top to clasp the head of his erection. Pulse here, contracting your pelvic floor again. Sliding back down, stop, and breathe each other in. Then repeat, as much or as little as you would like. Maintain power as you stay on top, ladies. Keep him, and yourself, on the brink of a mind-blowing climax. Don't let him dive off the edge until you're ready. By doing this, both of you will achieve an even greater orgasm when you finally succumb to ecstasy.

Role Playing

Role-playing enhances your sex life by encouraging you to use your imagination. So if dressing up floats your boat, then jump on that ship and damn well sail it. And for those of you that feel too shy to try this, it can be done without feeling like a cheesy film star. It really truly can. It can be simple - a personal trainer and client, doctor/nurse and patient, masseuse and client, teacher and student, home handy man and homeowner, call girl and rich businessman, or you can even pretend to be strangers. Or it can be a little more complex as you play roles of the dominator and the submissive – toys are loads of fun in this scenario (handcuffs and leg clamps anyone?). The possibilities are endless, and it lets you have fun dressing up if you want to go the whole hog. If you don't, it's okay to do this naked too. Just remember, it's all about feeling comfortable with what you're both doing, so talk about it, set limits and boundaries, and ease your way into it. And most importantly of all, have fun!

Strip Tease

Slowly undressing while your partner watches is the perfect way to increase arousal by megawatts. Add a little excitement by tying them to a bedhead or chair beforehand, and watch the desire-fuelled sparks fly. As with most of the Sex-Steps, ease into it. Jumpstart libidos with some slow sensual kissing and suggestive caressing first. But before you get carried away and rip each other's clothes off, stop, and take a step back. Stand before your lover, meet their gaze, and give them a front-row seat to the hottest strip show on earth. We're all sexy within our own right – so own it! Unzip, unbutton, or just tear clothes off, until piece-by-piece, you unravel your priceless goods. Playing some sexy music can help to ease any apprehensions and get you in the groove, as well as keeping the lighting low. Use toys, touch yourself, revel in the power you have as your lover watches on. And then reap the rewards when they finally get their hands on you.

Sacred Elixir Kisses

The two versions of this are extremely intimate and the perfect way to show just how much you're into one another. It may freak you out a little at first; if you've never broached this before, but give it a go…it's great for strengthening the bond between you.

Sacred Kiss 1

A whole new take on the good old 69er. You still do all the same moves and grooves, but once you've peaked and tumbled over that blissful edge together, it's time to turn right around and kiss, deeply. Savour each other's elixirs as you tongue tango. It's like enjoying an aperitif after a delectable dinner.

Sacred Kiss 2

Kiss. Ravish each other. Make hungry passionate love. Once you've both reached the pinnacle and fallen, making sure the man orgasms inside of you, he then slides down and licks some of his nectar from you. Then meeting you back at your lips, allow him to kiss you, slow and deep as you savour his taste. It's intensely satisfying.

Fantasy Finale

If you're game and ready to show your partner the fantasy/fantasies you wrote down at the beginning of this fun adventure, now's the time to do it. If you both choose to leave it hidden in your mind (or buried in the jar in the back yard) that's okay too. This is all about doing what's right for both of you. If you've followed each Sextion, and completed enough Sex-Steps, you would have no doubt strengthened the bond, reached a greater level of intimacy and fallen in love with each other all over again. If you both agree to go ahead with the big reveal, acting out your fantasies together is like the pot of gold at the end of the rainbow. There's also a possibility you've already fulfilled your fantasy through one of the Sex-Steps, and that's great too. Now is the time to let you're lover know this, and maybe you can make up a new fantasy, together. Whichever path you chose to take, support each other in your decision, and if you're going to act it out, have fun!

So there we have it, ladies and gents. You've made it to the final page. A big hurrah to you both! I hope you've had loads of fun with your lover/husband/wife along the way, learnt more about each other, got the fires of passion well and truly stoked, and through this sassy little book I've helped you to gain momentum in your sex life. Thank you, for trusting in me and grabbing yourselves a copy. If you have any questions, comments or simply just want to drop me a line, you can connect with me via my author FB page, or by email. I'd love to hear from you…

mandymagro75@hotmail.com
https://www.facebook.com/mandymagroauthor

Remember to stay grateful for one another, and to love each other with vigour. Life is too short for bad sex!

Love and best wishes,
Mandy Xo

www.ingramcontent.com/pod-product-compliance
Lightning Source LLC
Chambersburg PA
CBHW072113290426
44110CB00014B/1903